Oustau de Beaumanière

With special thanks to our photographers

Ditmar Bollaert
Vincent Gyselinck
Eric Morin
Patrick Verbeeck
Francis Vuillemin

&

Paul Kusseneers
Concept and Lay-Out

&

Printed by
A. De Cuyper-Robberecht n.v.

Compiled by Luc Quisenaerts
Concept and lay-out: Paul Kusseneers
Printed by : A. De Cuyper-Robberecht n.v.
Texts and English translation: Anne & Owen Davis
French translation: Philippe Bockiau & Philippe Françus
German translation: Eva & Hans-Jürgen Schweikart
Photos: see page 208
Publishers: D-Publications - Lier - Belgium

ISBN 90-76124-10-8   D/1998/8101/6

First Edition

Hidden gems of
PROVENCE

COMPILED BY

LUC QUISENAERTS

WRITTEN BY

ANNE & OWEN DAVIS

PUBLISHERS D-PUBLICATIONS

THE SERIES
hidden gems

Dear reader,

In this series, we take you to the most wonderful places to stay, to eat and to enjoy the specialities of a country, an area or a city.

Every article in this series is a journey of discovery, a unique revelation. We take a look behind the scenes in a hotel, a wine chateau, a restaurant where we savour the specialities of the chef or of the area....

With this series, we intend to give the readers the opportunity to leaf through each book and 'walk' through these wonderful spots, and discover the unique nooks and crannies of each of them.

Therefore this series, and each volume in itself, can be considered a valuable archive which brings a piece of the richness and beauty of an area or country into the home, created and cherished by the passion of the people who put part souls into it.

In word and photographs, the typical atmosphere of each place is conjured, and each book can be considered the 'key' to a wonderful and often undiscovered world.

The selection was made and approved of by the publisher himself, which guarantees it to be a unique experience, with unforgettable impressions of what our hosts have to offer.

Luc Quisenaerts
Publisher

Hidden gems of
PROVENCE

Hotels

The Provence is an ideal first choice for our series. Later, in books to follow, we will visit some of of the most beautiful restaurants in Europe, where each chef will tell us some of his secrets. But in this book, we are on a journey of discovery to find hotel gems, huddled - and often hidden - amongst the rocks of Les Alpilles, on the wide plains of the Camargue, in the greenery and the lavender fields of Lubéron, in the shadow of the papal palace in Avignon, under a radiant sun at the foot of Mont Ventoux and by the azure blue waters of the Mediterranean.

This will be a journey through the most beautiful 'mas' with their inviting swimming pools, but we will also visit hotels that once were convents or abbeys, age-old castles or stately manor houses. And wherever we go, there is always time to sit down under the trees, on shadowy terraces, to enjoy the scenery and the wonderful colours that are as enchanting now as when Gauguin, Van Gogh and Cézanne painted them.

THE COLLECTION

Château des Alpilles

The Alpilles are a range of rocky precitious hills that dominate the landscape. In Roman times, water was led by aqueducts to Arles and to the towns and villages in the surrounding countryside. The Pont du Gard is the most impressive, and even all these centuries later still stands as testimony to the expertise of those early Roman builders.

The Château des Alpilles is only a stone's throw away from those wild and romantic hills, in St. Remy-de-Provence. It was never strictly a 'château', but a great house that certainly deserves the name, and attached to it were extensive estates, a farm, vineyards, gardens, lakes, pastures and orchards.

In 1979, Jacques and Françoise Bon bought the château and made it into a four-star hotel. Its fortunes have gone with the fortunes of St. Remy itself, now a fashionable and much-visited town.

The hotel has been restored in a grand manner, both the main house and several of the buildings that constituted the farm. The lounges and the private suites and rooms are at once contemporary in their luxury and appointments, and traditional in the Provençal manner in all else: the warm and friendly interior and the gardens bear witness to a long and illustrious past.

A stay here is sheer luxury: there is nothing to do but enjoy yourself, the food is utterly delicious and the wine list extensive.

For those who want more action, tennis courts have been laid out alongside the swimming-pool; and ex-stunt man, Patrick Montomé, runs the Club Hippique in St. Remy and will escort parties horseback adventures deep into the Alpilles. François Bon offers exciting four-wheel drive forays into the undiscovered heart of the Camargue. And always, at the end of a long day, the welcoming Château des Alpilles is waiting to cosset you.

Hostellerie de Crillon le Brave

From high on its hilltop, Crillon le Brave has far distant and commanding views across the great expanse of typical Provençal countryside. Some 45 minutes north-east of Avignon, beyond the town of Carpentras, the road winds through seductive scenery and finally, at the highest point of the village from which the hotel takes its name, alongside the pretty church, the inviting portals of Crillon le Brave await.

Owners Peter Chittick and Craig Miller may hail from Toronto, but they have totally embraced the Provençal way of life. It all started in 1989, when they converted an old parsonage into a haven of rest and luxury, featuring 11 comfortable rooms. Later, they bought three adjoining buildings, added another 13 rooms and created the Crillon as it now is - a place of impeccable taste and refinement.

The hotel awakens in mid-March, just as the springtime almond blossom opens, and from then on, through the summer days, it is an ideal centre from which to immerse oneself in all the varied pleasures of the Provence- visits to vineyards of world renown, to potteries, art galleries, a profusion of wonderful street markets - where you may well encounter the hotel's chef purchasing the fresh vegetables, herbs and fruits he uses in his cuisine.

But a vacation is, most of all, an opportunity to rest and relax and the hotel is an ideal spot to do just that. The buildings and the deep-blue swimming-pool blend seamlessly into the Provençal landscape, but the cuisine is out of this world. It is fresh and aromatic, and if you have had the energy to go for a long hike, nothing will taste better than the aigo boulido, rich with garlic and succulent croutons.

Cloître Saint-Louis

An inscription in the chapel still shows her name: in 1589, Louise d'Ancézune made a donation to the Jesuits for the creation of a noviciate in Avignon. It took a hundred years and four architects to complete the monastery of Saint-Louis. Each generation added a personal touch: wings were built on, and bell towers, sculptured door frames, high vaulted galleries.

The Jesuits were not to enjoy Saint-Louis for very long. In 1768; French troops invaded Avignon and the Jesuits were banished from France.

In the years that followed, Saint Louis had a chequered history. Nuns turned it into a convent, wounded soldiers found a hospital bed under its roof, old people spent their last years there. From 1982 to 1987, the building stood empty.

Since then, Saint-Louis has found and dynamix lease of life. Today, a cultural centre and a luxury hotel live harmoniously under one roof. Hotel guests find their way down the long corridors, and the once spartan rooms have become luxurious suites. But the feeling of history, of many exciting lives led here, is still strong.

The hotel has 80 rooms and suites, and a swimming-pool… on the roof. Inside, everything is kept simple and minimalist, as if no piece of furniture should distract from the impressiveness of the vaulted corridors and the stone floors. Everything shows respect for the past: the wide venerable cloisters around the building still breathe the same serenity as in the time of those early Jesuits. The stone walls have been kept intact as much as possible, and are more decorative, somehow, than the most beautiful painting. The two contemporary wings are of a simplicity which is in perfect harmony with the original building, without trying to emulate it. And even after all those years, this is still a wonderful refuge for anyone who appreciates quiet and simple beauty. Some things never change.

A creation from one of France's most famous contemporary architects, Jean Nouvel.

Hostellerie La Grangette

We drive a dozen miles or so east from Avignon, tired after a day's sightseeing in the famous old town. Our destination, an hotel, spoken of in glowing terms, that had once been... a grain store, an ancient farm set deep in beautiful wooded countryside.

As we pull up outside the front door, it is abundantly clear that we will be very happy here. The house, built in the 19th century and later beautifully restored, sits comfortably on a hill, looking west towards the setting

sun. Highly colourful flowers grow profusely on every side and the lobby extends a friendly and charming welcome - more flowers, in vases, fruits displayed enticingly in baskets, soft lights and walls painted in warm and mellow colours. Brigitte and Jean Blanc-Brude, who completed the restoration in 1994, made it a home that exudes charm, colour and happiness.

A very original staircase with wrought iron railings leads up to the delightful guest rooms, fresh and full of light in the mornings, calm and warmly inviting by the evening light. Each of the 16 rooms has been charmingly personalised, set about with well-chosen antiques, and they all have fine views. Our room is decorated with a combination of sunny yellow Provençal materials, two large sunflowers hold back the curtains that half hide the view of the gorgeous countryside.

A stroll outside before dinner reveals a large and very inviting swimming pool set in a green glade…a perfect place for a siesta, and the hotel's gardens seem endless.

At dinner, at tables glinting with fine silver, we eat a wonderful meal and taste some of the delicate wines selected from nearby vineyards. Later, we enjoy a nightcap in the 'salon rouge' and decide that we are far too relaxed to make plans for tomorrow…

Le Moulin de Lourmarin

There are some places where you come only once in your life and you will never forget them. Such a place is Lourmarin, protected from the winds by the mountains of Lubéron. It has a beautiful renaissance castle, it has the grave of the famous French writer Albert Camus. And it has Le Moulin de Lourmarin, an hotel which is without doubt unique. An 18th century building that was once an oil mill, is now a jewel of four star comfort, where modern design and medieval architecture are combined in the most unusual way.

As soon as you enter, you feel that this is a special place. One side of the wonderful hall laid with large stone slabs, a spiral staircase winds up to the 20 rooms and two suites. Cast iron has been welded artfully into elegant balustrades, refined furniture and even four-poster beds, one of which we have in our own light and sunny room. Everything here is simple and modern, every detail has been chosen with great care. The window looks out over beautiful surroundings, and the water in the swimming pool shimmers invitingly. This is luxury of a superior kind.

The fairytale continues when we enter the dining room that evening, a gorgeous room with a domed ceiling and an impressive arched window looking out onto the garden. Even more impressive is the cuisine here, under the direction of talented young chef Edouard Loubet, who was awarded a Michelin star. He is a master in the use of wild herbs, picked in the surrounding countryside, and other fresh ingredients. Foie gras, seafood, succulent lamb such as we have never tasted before, regional cheeses and superior patisserie. Talk about a happy ending.

Domaine de Châteauneuf

Rich, famous and active in French politics he was, Louis-Maurice Châteauneuf. He was even an intimate of Napoleon Bonaparte. In the area it is claimed that the world ruler stayed on his domain, Châteauneuf, twice. Years and generations came and went and in 1919 Casimir Charles Châteauneuf was forced to sell the family domain for financial reasons. In 1926 the stately home was acquired by Fernand Malet, the master pâtissier of Toulon. His wife was an extraordinary cook and the couple turned the Domaine de Châteauneuf into a high quality 'auberge'. It is their children who gave the domain its present form and image and created one of the most famous hotels and restaurants of the area. Now the magnificent 18 hole Sainte-Baume golf course has been laid out in the splendid park like a garland around the hotel. The

Open Golf Club of France Group is the proud owner of this prestigious hotel. The Domaine de Châteauneuf is situated completely in the heart of Provence, slightly hidden behind the massif of La Sainte Baume, a beautiful but largely unknown part of Provence, and is a stone's throw not only from the Mediterranean but also from such places of interest as Aix-en-Provence and the city of Marseilles. If Napoleon had ever been given the chance to choose his place of exile, he would not have hesitated for a second...

Once, Napoléon Bonaparte was a guest at the 'Domaine de Châteauneuf'.

Le Mas de la Fouque

A verdant and flower-scented paradise in the expanses of the Camargue, Le Mas de la Fouque is the hotel for anyone whose curiosity has been aroused by those famous-ly romantic photographs of the wild white stallions galloping across the wilderness.

The horses are not, in fact, wild, but are overseen, by what we can, with a little lee-way, call cowboys. But they are not the whole story of the Camargue National Park - the wetlands are home, if only in the migration season, to scores of different birds - wild geese, ducks of every kind, herons, even pink flamingoes.

The hotel nestles right in the middle of this paradise, reached by a little sandy lane. As we arrive, we are greeted by shining white walls hung with a profusion of climbing roses. Luxurious vegetation embraces us wherever we look in the wide hotel grounds. The hosts, Jean-Paul Cochat and his wife Marthe, made it their passion to provide their guests with a sense of serene four-star luxury that perfectly mixes the natural beau-ties of the environment with tasteful and very original furnishings... such as the col-lection of antique guns on the walls and the ancient armoires in the lounges. The 14 air-conditioned rooms all have stunning views, some of the huge swimming-pool, others of flowery patios or the far reaches of the Camargue beyond.

The food is exquisite, with a choice of wines to match, but I will always remember my breakfast with special affection. As I sat by the pool sipping some excellent coffee, a fearless heron stepped out of the shadows and stood proudly nearby. Heaven could not be far away.

A guest in Mother Nature itself.

La Bastide

In an area such as the Provence, where time seems to have stood still and history can be felt everywhere, you wouldn't expect a modern building. That is why Hôtel La Bastide is such a surprise - and a pleasant one, we hasten to add.

In the heart of the Provençal landscape that great writers like Marcel Pagnol and Alphonse Daudet described with such love, lies Eygalières, like an old piece of jewellery, carefully preserved and lovingly polished from time to time, a beautiful, totally authentic village with winding streets and picturesque houses, where the inhabitants still have time for each other and the wafting scent of thyme, lavender and rosemary has not yet been replaced by the exhaust fumes of tourist coaches. And close to the village, set amongst olive groves and pine woods, the brand new Hôtel la Bastide can be found.

The hotel was built in 1992, and opened its doors in 1993. Nathalie Calabrese offers her guests all the creature comforts that can be expected from a modern hotel: the twelve fine rooms all have air-conditioning and cable television, and the water in the swimming pool is invitingly bright and blue.

And yet there are constant reminders that this is the Provence, for there are many traditional touches. The furniture is typical for the style of the area, the upholstery Provençal. This is a hotel to relax in, far from the stress of everyday life. But it is also a good starting point for endless trips in the environment: Arles and the eternally fasci-

nating Camargue are not far away, the road to Avignon is a stone's throw from here and the rocky footpaths of the Alpilles offer many wonderful walks. And then there is Eygalières itself, no more than ten minutes' walk from the hotel. Here, you find the best of both worlds, the romance of the old one and the comforts of the new one.

Jules César

Van Gogh is an indelible part, now, of the history of Arles, and his wonderful canvases have lent allure to our perceptions of the Provence. But the history of this beautiful region goes back centuries and its beauties, natural and architectural, rely on no one personage, however touched by genius.

In the middle of the 17th century, a convent was built for an order of the Carmelite nuns, who lived in their splendid edifice for over a hundred years, until by decree enclosed monastic orders were suppressed. Their buildings thenceforward housed orphans and the poor.

1929 saw the first hotel established here and today, after extensive refurbishments, the ancient buildings have reached new heights as the four-star Julius César, an hotel of considerable grandeur and quiet luxury.

But its owners have not forgotten that this was once a seat of religious quietude. As much of the past as possible has been retained. There are even some charming but very modest-sized rooms that were once nuns cells… and a graceful bell-tower, voiceless now, still rises into the sky.

Throughout the hotel, furniture and furnishings are antique, or take ancient designs for their inspiration. Curtains, cushions, wall-hangings - all are traditional.

After a day's sightseeing, it is wonderful to relax in the hotel's Provençal garden or the equally peaceful Cloister garden, both shaded by tall trees, and full of colourful flowerbeds. Call the barman over and order a long, refreshing drink, or cool off in the wonderful heated pool.

The hotel is justly proud of its cuisine, served in its 'Lou Marques' restaurant. In the hotel's kitchen, two top chefs and a patissier create culinary delights that will, in spite of the architectural splendours of Arles, be your best memory of a stay at the Jules César.

Hotel Jules César: a journey through more than 2,000 years of history in Arles.

La Cabro d'Or

La Cabro d'Or is sometimes called Oustau de Baumanière's little sister. And there is some truth in this: after all, the Cabro belongs to the same talented owner, Jean-André Charial, hotelier, wonderful chef and wine specialist. The Cabro also lies in the same wonderful environment: at the beginning of Devil's Valley, where Dante is said to have found inspiration for the hell in his Divine Comedy. A sunlit place where man's labour and nature's evolution together have created a landscape of abundance, with olive groves, almond trees, vines, a radiant blue sky and impressive rocky outcrops. Colours, shapes, aromas... Devil's Valley is one immense, slightly wild, and therefore irresistable garden.

On the road to-Oustau de Baumanière, lies La Cabro d'Or, a low, sunny building that has welcomed guests since 1961 in an atmospheric, relaxed environment. Its rooms and apartments open onto the garden and tradition and modernity combine in the refined, simple, but always tasteful decoration and furnishings. Both the garden and the sublime decoration are creations of Geneviève, the wife of Jean-André.

Here, every meal is a feast. Breakfast, served on the terrace under a bright white parasol; lunch, savoured around the swimming pool, and the evening meal, with wonderful gourmet food, made with the best and freshest local ingredients, prepared with respect for Provençal tradition and inspiration from far-away countries.

And then there is the environment. You can explore the area on horseback or by bicycle, play tennis or golf, take fascinating bicycle rides, visit fascinating museums and churches. The Camargue is close by; Nîmes and Avignon are within easy reach; Montpellier, Aix-en-Provence, Arles... there is so much to see. But there will be no better memory than the view from La Cabro d'Or of the green valley that once inspired Dante. Oustau's little sister proves that in some things, little sisters can be great!

Colours, aromas, and the southern ambiance.

Abbaye de Sainte Croix

The history of Abbaye de Sainte Croix goes back to the 4th century. According to legend, Saint Hilaire, archbishop of Arles, brought back from Palestine a piece of the cross of Christ. He founded the Chapel of the Holy Cross, high on a hill above Salon. The Abbey itself is known of since the IXth century, and has always been closely connected to the history of the nearby town of Salon. Hermits and religious communities lived here, the population came in procession to ask for holy intervention. But as the years went by, the Abbey became derelict. Then, in 1960, restoration works were started. In 1969 the Bossard family took over and slowly, with an endless care for detail, the old, crumbling abbey was transformed into a hospitable hotel that exuded an intense serenity. Cheerful oranges and sunny yellows chase every trace of sombreness from the vaulted rooms, a cosy fire glows in the imposing fireplace and in the guest rooms cast-iron lamps, made by local crafstmen,

throw muted light on the lovely interiors. As you gaze from your windows down across the green plains below, you feel completely at peace, and the everyday world seems very far away. But it is not just the wonderful building, the luxurious swimming pool and the gently wafting scent of thyme and savory that make a stay at The Abbaye de Sainte Croix such a unique experience; the cuisine is superior, and was rewarded the only Michelin star in the area. Savouring a fresh lobster, we try to imagine how, long ago, a certain Nicolas de Montgallet came here on a retreat, living on water and mouldy bread. It makes us glad that times have changed.

Staying here is like a journey back in time
to the 9th century.

Château de Montcaud

Halfway between the Cévennes and Avignon, surrounded by the vineyards of the Côtes du Rhône, stands a beautiful castle. For three years, Rudy W. Baur hunted all through France to find the ideal place for his dream hotel. He found it in 1990: the 19th century Château de Montcaud. It was more than love at first sight: the castle became his passion. He commenced restoration work, and from all over Europe collected items that would perfect the decoration: furniture, materials, crockery…

Today, Château de Montcaud is a dream come true. An imposing building, surrounded by a beautiful park with magnolias and pine trees, palm trees and cedars. Where once the French nobility spent its summers, privileged guests now stay in the utmost comfort. Inside, everything is tasteful and refined, in soft hues that match the surroundings perfectly: straw yellow, almond green, salmon pink…

Through the large windows in our room we look out onto the park, and for a minute, feel part of those days long gone… except for all the beautiful things that remind us of the comforts of the present: the heated swimming pool, the tennis court, the lovely restaurant where superior local cuisine is served.

In the basement, more 20th century luxury awaits: a fitness centre with sauna and a relaxing steam room. But we decide to take a walk in the park and discover a pond full of ducks and a strange grotto, in the romantic style of the 19th century. A stay here is a perfect combination of past and present, full of that special refinement that is timeless.

Château de Montcaud: once, the summer residence of the French landed aristocracy.

Le Mas d'Entremont

Le Mas d'Entremont is a sumptuously converted old Provençal farmhouse, a serene and dreaming hideaway not far from the vibrant artistic and cultural centre of Aix.

The rambling country house hotel is creeper-clad on the outside, full of heavy oak beams within - but the rooms are light and ariy with generous windows opening onto the wooded grounds, and balconies to step out onto to breathe the soft fresh airs of the morning.

Once settled in my air-conditioned room - there are 17 in all - the gardens and the beautiful clear-blue swimmingpool soon drew me outside again to explore. Soaring horse-chestnuts and tall, slim conifers provided deep and welcome shade from the afternoon heat. Another pool, with floating creamy-coloured water-lilies and dancing fountains, invited me to rest awhile and watch the contented goldfish slide. There were lush lawns, a tennis court, quiet courtyards with huge stone urns spilling with blood-red geraniums.

But notwithstanding all that beauty, it was the cuisine at Le Mas d'Entremont that was the most memorable of all. The menu allowed plenty of choice. I decided on chef's Thierry Bongrand's specialities and began with mussels in a saffron sauce, followed by monkfish stuffed with basil. The cheese basket was decorated with sprigs of rosemary and I chose a local Provençal Banon - a creamy goat's cheese. There is an excellent Beaujolais, and the hotel is well-known for its delicious patisserie. On this long warm summer evening, I dined on the terrace, which overlooks the waterlilies and serenely splashing fountains.

A home from home, almost, but few of us would recognise our own home, except in the welcoming and cozy atmosphere.

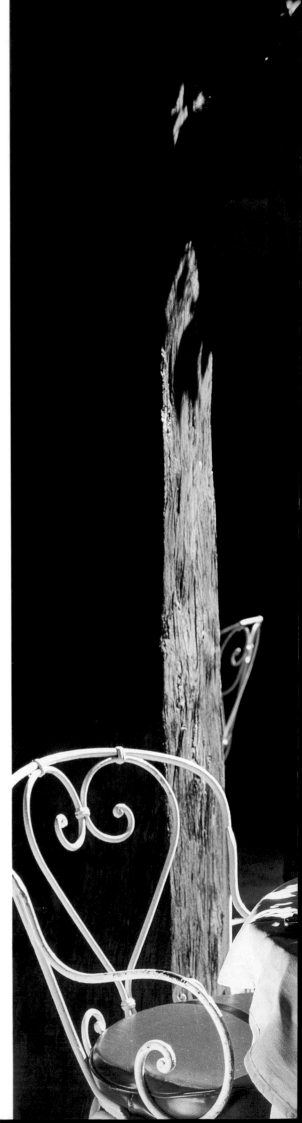

An oasis of romance.

Le Mas de Peint

The Camargue, with its fascinating marshland and its wonderful flora and fauna, has always been a magical place. When you travel here, you feel very far removed from day to day life, and find yourself dreaming of being part of this very different world, if only for a while.

That dream becomes luxurious reality at Le Mas de Peint, where Jacques Bon and his wife Lucille have created a hospitable home that is unique of its kind.

Jacques grew up in the Rhône delta, where he grows rice and breeds merino sheep and Camargue bulls. The house, which was built for Antoine Peint in the 17th century, has been property of the Bon family for generations. It was Lucille, an architect, who had the idea to open the house to travellers, and the Mas took on a new lease of life.

Together with interior architect Estelle Réale-Garcin, Lucille created an oasis of light and refinement, but kept the authenticity of the house intact. Guests take their meals at a large round antique table in the kitchen, and the lounge is like a family living room. But there is also a luxurious swimming pool, and the guest rooms are immaculate, tasteful and extremely comfortable.

The greatest adventure of all is the Camargue itself. Jacques likes taking his guests out in a four-wheel drive vehicle to explore the environment, or if you want to be a cowboy for a day, you can ride into the Camargue on horseback. Either way, you'll be in silent admiration at the sight of the innumerable wild flowers, the strange elegant pink flamingoes, the wild white horses. A holiday at Le Mas de Peint is a unique experience.

This is the world of Jacques Bon.

Mid-way between Nimes, Uzès and Avignon is the ancient and pretty little village of Collias, hidden in the lavender blues of the glorious countryside. And Collias itself hides a further secret: behind a tall, imposing ochre-coloured façade that seems to have absorbed the warmth and colour of the southern sunlight, is an hotel of magical charm.

Le Castellas is the creation of Chantal and Raymond Aparis. They have drawn together several ancient buildings around a palm-shaded inner courtyard - and the whole of it is a work of art, full of wonderful touches and surprises. Each of the 15 rooms and two suites has its own style: art deco, art nouveau, the seventies... There is an an Egyptian room with a view from its private

terrace, overlooking the rooftops of Collias... and - you'll have to believe me - a bath and shower open to the skies! Spectacularly beautiful is the bathroom designed and built by sculptor Jules Guilbert, with a pebbled floor and bath, and a wonderful mirrored ceiling.

The interior patio is a secret world of luxury and peacefulness. Large parasols invite

Hostellerie Le Castellas

you to just sit and enjoy the silence, shaded from the sun. The gardens are suggestive of Monet's, full of unexpected corners, light and shade, and a venerable wisteria that provides a tunnel of soft green where tables have been placed and visitors can sip tea and relax.

There is a wide blue swimming-pool waiting to be discovered, and as evening decends,

the vaulted, stone-floored but friendly-looking restaurant will welcome you. Chef Frédéric Fournier creates a diverse, light and tasty cuisine that uses the freshest of vegetables and fruit drawn from the immediate Provençal countryside. Heavenly - like everything about Le Castellas.

Fairy-tale charm full of surprises.

Hostellerie du Vallon de Valrugues

If we could choose one term to describe Hostellerie du Vallon de Valrugues, it would be 'joie de vivre'. Here, you feel that life is sweet, that the sun of Provence shines just for you and that a little too much of a good thing is not always bad.

As soon as you arrive, you feel like a privileged guest: a monumental staircase with an impressive baldaquin leads to the entrance of a Florentine-style villa full of colours and hospitality. Real marble lives here next to trompe d'oeil decorations, painted flowers and frescoes, and upstairs, a red carpet leads to the hotel room doors of the same red, each marked with an elegant V. The rooms themselves are exquisitely decorated with an abundance of Provençal materials and wood, french windows lead to a sunny balcony. High over the rooftops, almost, in would seem, in the sky, is a magnificent 'royal suite' which boasts its own private swimming pool.

The dining room with its splendid chandeliers, the extravagant but attractive piano bar and the wonderful cuisine: Valrugues is certainly worthy of its four stars. If you want to enjoy the sunshine, the scents of the trees and the flowers in the park, and still protect yourself from the sometimes fickle wind and the intensely bright light of the country, there is the magnificent terrace surrounding a luxurious swimming pool.

The hotel is described as: "A bit of Italy in the land of the mistral, a combination of the sunny, sometimes exuberant south and the softness of the landscape of Saint-Rémy."

A winning combination, that is for sure.

A Florentine-like villa in the heart of Provence.

103

Château Unang

This château with the intriguing name lies at the foot of Mont Ventoux, just outside Luberon. A long, curving avenue takes us through the thickly forested countryside until we arrive before the solemn and majestic creeper-covered façade of Château Unang itself.

We pull up in the wide gravelled courtyard and admire the classic simplicity of the great building, its elegant towers, its antique wrought iron gateway and the geometric gardens around us.

The interior is no less of a pleasure: imposing tall-ceilinged rooms with pieces of antique furniture, paintings and tapestries on the walls and curtains and covers in typical Provençal designs. And yet, here and there, are homely touches that tell of the warmth and friendliness that await guests at Château Unang: the scents of cooking that escape from the open kitchen door, the pile of baskets in the hallway that have transported bottles of wine from surrounding vineyards, the thick cosy towels laid ready for us in our bathroom.

One cannot help feeling special in such a place. And our own particular room, 'La Chambre du marquis', finished in a soft rosé pink and almond green, with a wonderful Louis XVI bed, will be something we'll remember for a long time.

And the hotel's name? I looked up the history of the house, which took me as far back as the year 867, and led me through the centuries to 1970, when our current hosts M. and Mme Lefer undertook the extensive restoration that made Unang the jewel it is today… and I was still no wiser as to its origin. But with Marie-Hélène Lefer's seductive cuisine to engage me and my choice to be made from no less than 60,000 bottles in the Unang's cellar, I understood that, whatever its name, a rose will always smell as sweet!

Oustau de Baumanière

The Oustau is more than an hotel, it is a philosophy of life. A place of refinement and good taste, which respects the traditional but at the same time embraces the modern, set in a glorious landscape, where the sun is always shining. In other words: the perfect place for a restful holiday, in one of the most beautiful parts of Provence.

The hotel is situated in the rocky, herb-scented Alpilles, at the foot of a dramatic outcrop topped by an old and romantic château.

The Oustau de Baumanière was built back in 1634 and has been an hotel now for over 50 years. Each of the 12 luxurious rooms and eight apartments has its own unique and charming character but all of them open out onto the attractive gardens, full of the play of shadows and light, with long views of the countryside beyond.

The gardens provide not only a visual feast and a haven of peace for the traveller, but its richly varied produce - fruits, vegetables and herbs of all kinds - are an immediate source of fresh food for the chef's irresistable gourmet treats. The same flair for refinement and grace that inspired the design of the surroundings is apparent, too, at the table. Perhaps this is not surprising, for Jean-André Charial, unusually, is both head chef and the proprietor. From his kitchen come the most delicate of dishes, each of them a work of art, a feast for all the senses. Some of the nicest wines served at Oustau come from the vineyard nearby - but that is another story, because when you live in the Provence, own two hotels and are a gourmet chef, you will inevitably be fascinated by wine. That certainly goes for Jean-André Charial, who owns both Oustau de Baumanière and Cabro d'Or. His passion for wines dates from the eighties, and slowly, he developed an ambition to create his own wine.

115

In 1988 he associated himself with Jean-Pierre Peyraud, who had just purchased the Mas de Romanin and his first acres of old vines. Together, they developed Château Romanin, a vineyard that now produces some wonderful wines.

Since 1989 Romanin is cultivated according to biodynamic methods: no synthetic chemicals are used, and everything is based on the four fundamental elements of earth, water, air and heat. 12 different vines, each with their own character, are combined into wines that perfectly reflect the area they come from. Honest, generous and simple, aromatic, full-bodied and yet refreshing.

There are red wines, of which the Château Romanin is the most important. A beautiful ruby-red wine with a purple sheen, made from hand-picked grapes, which can be kept 10 years and more. Or the Chapelle de Romanin, deep red with a violet glow, tasting of fruits of the forest and spices, with fine tannins. The salmon-red rosé is fresh and fruity, the white Château Romanin with its yellow colour and green sheen is a harmonious wine in which you can taste all the goodness of Provence. When you stay at Oustau de Baumanière or Cabro d'Or, look for these wonderful wines on the wine list. Your host will serve them with a smile.Pablo Picasso, Kirk Douglas, Georges Pompidou, even Queen Elizabeth II… at first sight they seem to have very little in common, apart, of course, from the fact that they are famous. But one other common factor between them is that they have all been guests at Oustau de Baumanière.

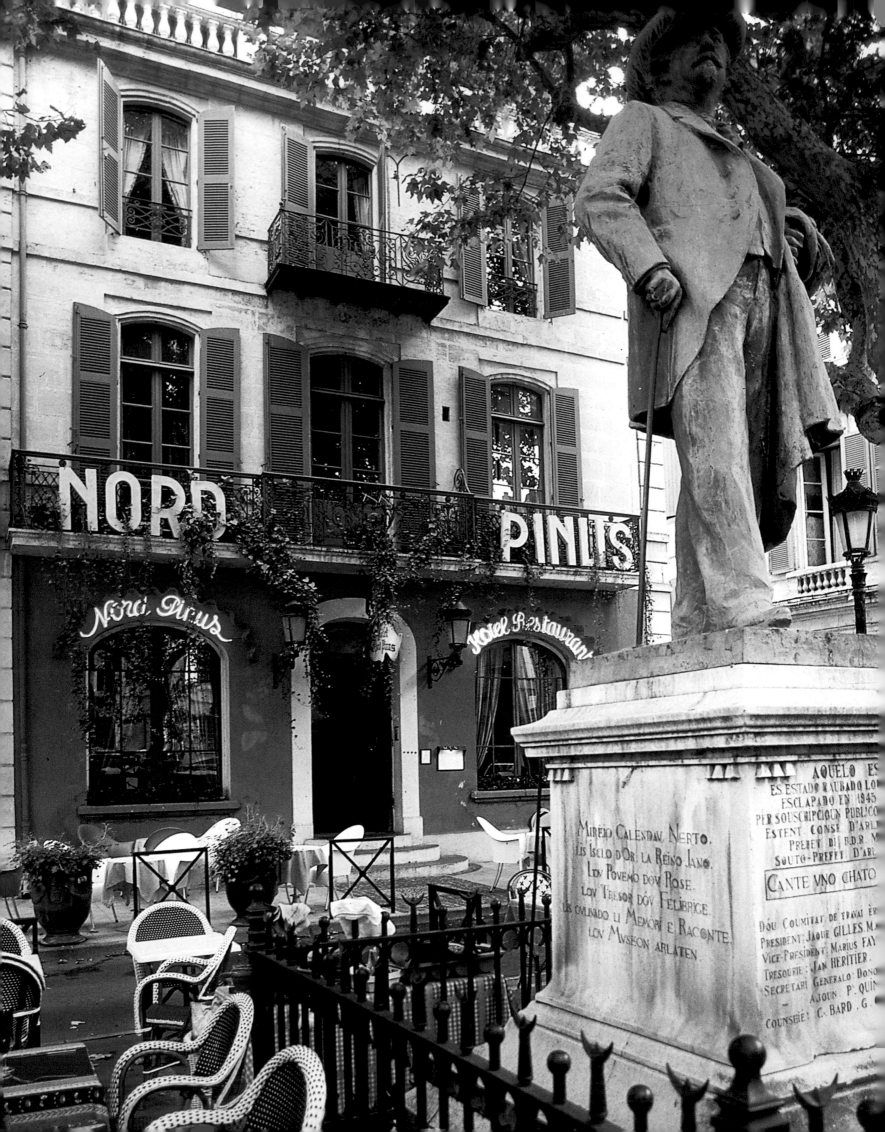

Grand-Hôtel Nord Pinus

Mention Arles and immediately the name of Van Gogh comes to mind. But the town boasts many other associations with famous personages… and most of them have stayed at the Grand Hotel Nord-Pinus. Picasso caroused in the hotel bar 'La Cintra' during the annual bullfights. Henry James, Jean Cocteau, Simone Signoret, Peter O'Toole and the successive nameless heroes of the bullring, have all stayed here.

The Nord-Pinus, on the Place du Forum in the heart of Arles, first opened its doors in 1865. It soon became a mecca for the artistic and the fashionable, and has remained so ever since, apart from a melancholy hiatus in the late seventies and early eighties.

Under the nostalgic vision of Anne Igou, the totally restored Nord-Pinus has reclaimed all its old allure - and more. The airy comfortable rooms are beautifully furnished with antiques and delicate, ornate wrought-iron bedsteads, the lounges decorated with fascinating life-size papier-mâché figures and old bullfighting posters.

You don't have to go far to find a superior place to eat. Attached to the hotel is the Brasserie Nord-Pinus, intimate and homely with its far honey-coloured candles and blue-and-white checked tablecloths, offering a short but high-quality menu, with fine wines.

Arles is a town with plenty to offer the visitor, especially its museums and its colourful vibrant markets, but it is also a convenient centre for visits to the reedy marshlands of the Camargue, some 40 minutes by car, and the wonderful beaches of the Mediterranean coast.

Picasso was also addicted to the exceptional
charisma of this hotel.

120

Auberge de Cassagne

Staying in the Provence means immersing yourself in a whole way of life, finding a warm welcome in a place that respects the traditions of the area. We find such a welcome at the Auberge de Cassagne, a four-star hotel in the shadow of the castle of Cassagne. The lovely building dates from 1850, but it was not until 1983 that Françoise and Jean Michel Gallon bought it and made it into a gem amongst hotels. It has 29 rooms, 5 apartments and a luxurious suite, each tastefully and harmoniously furnished in the materials and the colours of the area. Equally harmonious is the way top chef Philippe Boucher works together with sommelier André Trestour, combining superior regional cuisine with luxurious and exquisite wines. Life is wonderful in this place, romantic, relaxing.

But in the Provence, the great outdoors alway beckons. The radiant blue swimming pool shimmers, the loungers invite you to stretch out and enjoy the sunshine. In the children's pool, a little girl splashes around; a man clad in whites passes by on his way to the tennis court. We choose to play jeu de boules -this is the Provence, after all- and later relax our tired muscles in the jacuzzi. There is a splendid dining, but tonight, we dine on the terrace, under age-old plane trees. Invisible crickets chirp their happiness. As we sip our wine, we couldn't agree with them more.

Your stay here is like immersing yourself in
the unique ambiance of the Provence.

127

Château d'Arpaillargues

In a little village three miles outside Uzès, set apart from the world behind thick and severe-looking walls, the historical Château d'Arpaillargues is full of the sweet and secret charm of a Provençal mansion. Built in the 15th century on the site of an even older medieval edifice, the château was restored first in the 18th century, then more recently, to exacting standards, as a wonderfully romantic luxury hotel that breathes history and a refined peacefulness. The sea coast, the Cévennes and the Camargue are a scant half-hour's drive away - there is much to discover here, much to enjoy. And at the time of the festivals, this part of the Provence becomes one big adventure, a wonderful event for locals and tourists alike.

Delicious food and excellent wines are offered in the vaulted dining-rooms of the hotel, where cozy log-fires crackle in the shadowed fire-places, and on warm summer evenings, under tall trees in the candlelit castle courtyard.

After your meal, wander into the 2 _ acre gardens and watch the rising moon playfully reflected in the turquoise pool.

There are two luxury apartments and 25 tastefully furnished rooms. Bring your raquets and your golf clubs: the hotel has tennis courts and there are fine golf courses a stone's throw down the road. But there is more: the Gardon Calode is a wonderful place for canoeing and kayaks, Uzès has the most fascinating museums and lovely shops full of arts and crafts.

History, culture, gourmet food and sheer luxury combined with exquisite taste - the Château d'Arpaillargues has it all. No wonder so many of the guests return time and again, to enjoy the magic of the place.

Hôtel du Général d'Entraigues

Conveniently set in the heart of the ancient Provençal town of Uzès, the Hotel du Général d'Entraigues is nevertheless a peaceful and secluded hideaway, with a history going back to the 15th century. Once the home of an influential noble family, it has now been sumptuously restored as an hotel of considerable elegance and charm, offering every modern comfort.

Our air-conditioned room is gracefully furnished and offers a stunning view over the old rooftops of Uzès. The choice is difficult here: explore the environment, or take advantage of the many facilities the hotel itself has to offer: the swimming-pool, the fitness room with jacuzzi and solarium? We decide to do both, and wander through the delightful streets of beautiful Uzès, looking in antique shops, admiring the Cathedral and the wonderful bell-tower. Then we return to the hotel, where we have a leisurely swim and relax in the sauna. After that, it is time for dinner, and new choices need to be made.

There are two dining rooms: the 'Jardins de Castille' providing first class gourmet food, served on the delightful and romantic terrace in the summer, and also 'Le Bain Bouche', serving pancakes and salads, an appetising buffet featuring Provençal delicacies and a cosy tea room. We opt for the terrace and dine by candlelight.

The Hotel d'Entraigues is a home from home, where you feel pampered and cared for in a stunning environment. For stunning it is: the view from the terrace, the pretty countryside, the wonderful scents of the Provence. And then there is the invariably sunny weather, which will remind you that this is not home after all, but a place with a far more friendly climate.

131

Hostellerie Les Frênes

Avignon. The very name sets the heart dreaming of sunshine, history, and romance. Of a river too, of course, wide and green, flowing south into the fabled Mediterranean. The reality does not disappoint, rather the opposite - it fills all the gaps that poor imagination left unfilled.

Just a few minutes beyond the walls of Avignon is the historic Hostellerie Les Frênes, a pefect home from home when visiting Provence.

The beautifully-proportioned house was built in 1810 and restored as an hotel by Jacques Biancone in 1969. In 1975, Jacques and his wife Elyane could only offer eight bedrooms, but already their hotel was awarded four stars. Today there are 22 luxurious rooms and in 1987 a Michelin star was added to their clutch of awards.

The hotel is very much a family affair. Eldest son Hervé Biancone is manager and Antoine, the youngest, is head chef and one of the most celebrated of his generation, already gathering an international reputation.

Outside, manicured lawns, tall trees and a beautiful swimming pool where on sunny mornings, breakfast become an unforgettable event. Inside, the lounges and bedrooms are warm, relaxing and luxurious. Antoine's cuisine, in the hotel's Jardin des Frênes, is everything his repute would lead you to expect - original, lively and very tasty indeed.

I sat down in the beautifully-appointed dining-room and began with a cassolette d'escargots, followed by a fish course with wonderful pistou. My stuffed pigeon was accompanied by fresh pasta redolent of truffle, and a pungent goat's cheese with a mild cinnamon touch was a perfect finale. I took my coffee on the front terrace and listened to the sound of cicadas. When I stood up to leave, an owl hooted close by. It was as if my arrival here were being celebrated by the whole of Provence's natural world…

Top class, just outside the centre of Avignon.

Château de la Pioline

There are many old hotels in the Provence, but this may well be the oldest - although much changed as the years went by, even its name. In 1301, the 'Moulin de Verdaches' was built on the banks of the river Arc, not far from the centre of Aix-en-Provence. Later, it was renamed 'Beauvoisin', and in 1616 the castle became the property of the Piolenc family, who gave it its final name. Various owners left their stamps on the castle - and then came the day when the furniture was sold, the rooms were locked, and the grounds at last deserted. Even the most beautiful of castles will crumble when man neglects them.

In 1987, Josette en André Armand bought Château de La Pioline - on a whim. It was not until later that they decided to make it into an hotel. Whoever stays there now, will be grateful for their decision.

Today, ferns and wild flowers bloom around the castle, and benches invite the visitor to sit down awhile and enjoy the scenery. The house itself has been beautifully restored, with the help of local craftsmen. Josette Armand, together with interior architect

Jean de Petit-Tresserves, have filled the rooms with splendid furniture, paintings and mirrors, with glittering silverware and wonderful crockery, and bed and bath linen of superior quality.

Each of the 21 rooms and suites of the Château has something special to offer: one looks out over the grounds towards the swimming-pool and club house, another has its own private garden. But wherever you stay in this castle, one of the highlights will certainly be the evening meal. Chef Christophe Gillino prepares wonderful dishes, some of them full of surprising contrasts, others with a perfect harmony of different elements - like the Château de La Pioline itself.

Inspired by the passion of Josette and André Armand for the past.

145

Les Roches

In a spectacular setting, at Aiguebelle, on the Provençal coast, perched high on a rocky cliff overlooking the Mediterranean, Les Roches is an hotel in a league of its own. Far out across the sea are the Îles d'Or, the golden isles of Porquerolles, and down the coast just a little way is the chic St. Tropez… and beneath the cliffs, moored at the private landing-edge, is the hotel's own boat, ready to take you there. Behind the hotel, all the glorious countryside of Provence beckons.

But even with so much choice, you could be excused for neglecting it all, in favour of the oasis of calm and serenity that is Les Roches itself. Its comfortable lounges, discreet and charming bar, its wonderful rooms and elegant suites, furnished with the finest of Provençal antiques and opening onto balconies with wonderful views… Why trouble to go anywhere, when just outside your door lie exotic gardens full of cactus, palms, oleanders and hibiscus that clothe the steep hillsides right down to the azure swimming pool, the private beach and the lapping waves of the warm enticing sea.

And who would want to miss lunch, served at the water's edge in the romantic, sun-drenched beach restaurant, watching the comings and goings of yachts and cabin cruisers? The simple plates of delicately prepared local fish and seafood are unforgettable. In the evening, the soft-lit ambiance of the hotel's main restaurant is an ideal setting in which to enjoy the rare culinary treats and fine wines for which Les Roches is justly celebrated.

The guest book is filled with famous names - Liz Taylor and Richard Burton stayed here, Christian Dior and Thomas Mann. They all must have realised what a wonderful hideaway Les Roches can be.

This is also Provence.

The sensation of staying on a luxury yacht.

Auberge de Noves

In the heart of Provence, in 15 acres of parkland thickly scattered with pines and oak trees, stands a 19th-century manor house. If you half close your eyes and breathe in the wonderful scents, you can imagine how once, genteel mothers might have walked along these paths with their white-clad little daughters, and how, perhaps, a lonely young lady with a secret love once planted her easel here and made a melancholy watercolour painting of her surroundings.

The peace and the scents still abound, but melancholy is nowhere to be found now. These days, Auberge de Noves is a wonderful hotel, rewarded with several Michelin stars. A family business, for since Robert and Suzanne Lalleman first opened the house to travellers in 1955, Lallemans have always been in charge here.

Robert and Suzanne were a perfect team: he had endless plans and ideas, the kind of man who sets a flower on the breakfast tray; she combined practical insight with refined taste. Together, they made the Auberge de Noves a place where life is good, a restful hideaway for anyone who feels a need to wind down, sit back awhile and listen to the quiet voice of nature.

Nowadays, André Lalleman and his wife are in charge. And once again, they complement each other perfectly; she gives the house that typical Provençal touch, he is the ideal host. After many years in Europe, their son Pierre II has returned home and is now in command of the kitchen.

You can simply stroll in the wonderful landscape that stretches out in every direction. But you can also play tennis, or petanque, or table tennis. There is a heated outside pool, and a golf course close by. If you wish, you can even go hunting, or admire the beautiful scenery from a helicopter. But the best,

maybe, awaits you at the end of the day, in the form of a gastronomic meal prepared, with impeccable taste, by Pierre Lalleman. Or perhaps even later, when, from the window of your luxurious room, you watch the sun set on the Provence.

La Bastide de Capelongue

A small, elegant and extremely charming hotel, La Bastide de Capelongue in the Vaucluse offers the fortunate visitor stunning views over the romantic rooftops of the tiny nearby village of Bonnieux.

At the foot of the village, a lazily flowing tree-lined river twinkles in the morning; a church-bell chimes; a cat winds itself around the legs of my poolside chair, as I sip my coffee, then seats itself beside me, as if to also enjoy the view.

La Bastide was opened in April 1997, but already it has acquired a wonderful reputation. The entire hotel is so artfully decorated and furnished that one feels one might be in a living gallery. Each room has its own special, cosy feel and its own particular examples of fine furnishings and original materials. Classically Provençal or shamelessly romantic, each of them is exquisite in its own way. Small details, like the lavender-filled embroidered pillows that serve as room-key holders, make this hotel such a wonderful place to stay.

I set out to explore Bonnieux and its environment. At the small outdoor market, I taste wonderful ripe fruit and admire colourful local vegetables. In l'Isle-sur-la-Sorgue, I wander around the beautiful antique shops and stop for another coffee and some people-watching. Tormorrow, I may visit Arles and Nîmes, or maybe I'll head for Avignon to see if the famous bridge is still there.

Later, in the wonderful light dining room of the hotel, after an exquisite meal, I savour the regional cheeses. The menu is inspired by the son of the owners, chef Edouard Loubet, the youngest in the land to be awarded a Michelin star . It's easy to understand why…

Villa Gallici

In Aix-en-Provence with her plethora of noble mansions built centuries ago with golden yellow stones and sculpted splashing fountains in the center of several town squares, two interior decorators, Gil Dèz and Charles Montemarco, together with Daniel Jouve, have transformed an 18th century manor house into an elegant and luxurious hotel with 22 very distinctive and elegant rooms.

Decorated with the warmth and charm of the Provence, the influence of Italy and Great-Britain, each room opens to either a terrace or private garden and lies only a short distance from the villa's small but serenely beautiful swimming pool, situated in a Florentine-style garden surrounded by magnificent old cypress trees.

Maintained in the French tradition by a staff of dedicated housekeepers wearing frilly white eyelet petticoats, the villa is immaculate, the attention to detail extraordinary.

In addition to polishing the numerous silver cachepots, straightening pictures that hang from taffeta ribbons and fluffing up curtains that tend to puddle on the floor, the staff also can be found from time to time applying the essence of lavender into the carpets, providing the hallways and public areas with a scent that has long been synonymous with the region.

Wrought-iron garden furniture and shade trees fill the villa's idyllic terrace, the picture-perfect setting for breakfast, lunch and dinner which, weather permitting, are also served on occasion by the tranquil and picturesque pool.

Attention to detail is exceptional, thanks to the dedicated staff.

Le Relais de la Magdeleine

It had been a hot day, one of the hottest of the Provençal summer, but now the sun was sinking behind the hills, and I was seated at a table twinkling with silver cutlery, sipping an unfamiliar but excellent local wine and consulting the menu. A cool breeze wafted through the orangerie, whose other diners were also taking their places. I allowed myself the luxury, just for a while, of feeling special, one of a chosen few.

But here, at Relais de la Magdeleine, hosts M. and Mme. Marignane have worked with a passion to foster just this feeling of being special in their guests, so it is no delusion after all. This is a wonderful place: the hotel stands in peaceful tree-shadowed gardens, set about with 18th century statues, an inviting swimming-pool; a wide and lovely terrace, where the sound of splashing fountains is never far away. Louis XIII furniture decorates the lounge, and the grand dining-room boasts delicate parquet and marquetry. A majestic staircase leads up to rooms of great luxury with marble bathrooms. My own room had a wonderful, light-hearted trompe-l'oeil beneath the wide windows and wall-paintings cleverly executed in the 18th century style.

Back in the gastronomic orangerie, it was high time I made my choices. I was offered the charming assistance of Mme Marignane herself, and was soon enjoying the chef's tasty soup of freshly-picked Provençal vegetables and looking forward to a main course of lamb and, I was promised, many secret ingrediënts.

The Relais de la Magdeleine is a place one might be tempted also to keep a secret, were it not already a long-established hotel, opened in 1935, with a wide and deserved reputation for fine food, a quality cellar and a serene and friendly atmosphere.

171

The dining room has a magnificent parquet floor and marquetry, and a wide staircase leads to the luxury rooms.

La Mirande

In a quiet cobbled street in Avignon, opposite the Papal palace, stands a dream hotel that is really far too special to be called 'hotel'. Behind its pale yellow façade lies a world of refinement and luxury.

The 17th-century building was once a cardinal's palace, and the present owners, the Steins, have made La Mirande their life's work. Their son Martin even gave up his medical studies to concentrate on its restoration. Together with architect François-Joseph Graf he collected documentation and old materials: tiles, stones, antique window panes. Slowly, with the help of craftsmen, ironmongers and painters, the atmosphere of a family home from times long gone was recreated. The wood panelling, the staircase with its ornamental railing, the pink-ochre patina on the restaurant walls and the magnificent 15th century ceiling - everything has been carefully thought out. They scoured old collections to find the most beautiful wallpapers and the most fascinating upholstery to decorate the rooms, which arc Provençal, with the odd eastern touch. To all this, the Steins have added unique pieces of furniture, wall-hangings and objects that they found on their travels.

The result is a magical mix of styles and eras, shapes and memories.

The nineteen rooms are each different, but every detail has been chosen to delight the guests. The bathrooms, with their marble baths and traditional English taps, are sheer luxury.

As could be expected, the cuisine is both refined and delicious, and if you want to learn the tricks of the trade from chef Daniel Hébet, you can take a course, held in the basement kitchen, where the white tiles come from a brasserie in Marseille and the shelves arc filled with Provençal crockery. With his recipes, you can take a piece of La Mirande home with you - and still savour the memories.

The 17th century building was once the palace of a cardinal.

A world of sophistication and luxury.

Le Mas de l'Oulivié

At the base of the village of Les Baux-de-Provence, hidden among olive trees, lies an hotel that has created its own, breath-takingly beautiful setting. Mas de l'Oulivié may have been recently built, but it has nestled itself so perfectly in its surroundings that it seems to have been there forever.

As soon as you enter the spacious reception area, you feel at home here. Everything is light and pleasant, decorated with impeccable taste and a great respect for traditional architecture. The terra cottatiles on the floor are hand made, the roof tiles are old and the façade features stone from Les-Baux-de Provence. The house itself, in light sand stone and with shutters of the palest almond green, exudes peace and cosiness.

Our room is a pleasant surprise: light colours, rustic furniture made by well-known local designers, and everywhere the materials the Provence is famous for. Urgé

materials, based on old Provençal prints, and in the suite the latest materials from the Souleïado collection.

But the most beautiful of all is the swimming pool, which seems to spring from its surroundings like a real oasis. Rocks, a pebble beach, a jacuzzi - and inviting loungers. Can you imagine a better place to enjoy the colours and the overwhelming scents that are so typical of the Provence?

We enjoy the view of the wonderful gardens, and savour a delicious salad, richly sprinkled with the olive oil from the Mas, which has its own appellation. It is first class - like everything else here.

At the foot of Les Alpilles, a hotel has created its own breathtaking setting.

Le Mas de la Brune

Le Mas de la Brune, set in the very heart of Provence, on the edge of a splendid village a little north-east of Arles, is a beautifully proportioned, classic Renaissance castle, built for the Isnard family in 1572. The building is a fascinating mix of mildly defensive architecture - a watchtower, small ground-floor windows - playful ornamentation, and comfortably familial touches. Pagan legends and the Gospel itself formed the inspiration for the decorative motifs found on the façade. This was very obviously once the home of a rich, religiously-inclined family who did not really expect agression.

Step in through the heavy, oak front door and the interior, too, is a delight - elegant stone-vaulted rooms, sonorous with antique gravity yet prettily furnished seem to glow with a relaxed and generous happiness.

At La Brune, you live as if you were in a museum, but one that pulses with life and friendliness. Our room, decorated in the romantic style of the area, has warm terracotta walls and a wonderful four-poster bed. The Provençal scents of lavender and roses seem to envelop us as we throw open a mullioned window, breathe in the southern air, and listen to a soft breeze shuffle the leaves of ancient chestnut trees.

The glorious swimming pool shimmers invitingly. But after a few laps, the deckchairs surrounding the pool are even more inviting and as we lie soaking up the sun, we feel as if we have been set down in paradise.

Later, over drinks by the magnificent open fire, we decide to have a meal in the village. What better way to enjoy the wonderful scents of herbs and plants, and listen to the sounds of the crickets, than on a leisurely walk with a beautiful meal waiting at the end.

A jewel of a renaissance castle, bathed in luxury.

Le Bistrot d'Eygalières

One of the greatest pleasures of travelling is enjoying an authentic meal, prepared with local ingredients. And in the Provence, this means; fresh fish, tender lamb, fresh vegetables - and the many wonderful herbs that the area provides: thyme, sage, savory.

When we asked the friendly owners of Le Mas de la Brune the name of a good restaurant, their advice turned out to be quite a surprise. For dining at the Bistrot d'Eygalières means: savouring the best that Provence has to offer - prepared by a chef from west Flanders.

This restaurant, named after the beautiful village it stands in, is run by Suzy and Wout Bru. They met at the hotel school in Bruges where they studied for six years. Suzy specialised in wines and reception, Wout made the kitchen his speciality. They worked in many renowned restaurants in Flanders, London and the Provence, and in 1995 they decided to start their own business. The Bistrot was awarded a Michelin star in 1998, which shows just how successful they have become.

The façade of the bistro is like a village café. But inside, everything is of superior taste, and it is not surprising that Suzy and Wout have built up a regular gourmet clientele. Wout's cuisine is light and refined, with a perfect technique and a wonderful feeling for the right amount of herbs and spices. A cuisine that is something between classic

and spontaneous, but always with great respect for local produce. A savoury tart with fresh sardines, roast pigeon with foie gras, brioche with truffles, lamb with sage... you are spoilt for choice here. But one thing to bear in mind: you absolutely must save some space for the wonderful desserts. A millefeuille with orange mousse, chocolate and wild rasberries for instance. Delightful.

USEFUL INFORMATION

LE CHÂTEAU DES ALPILLES

- **Room amenities:** 15 double rooms (each different from the others) in the castle + 4 suites and apartments in the farmhouse (modern country style).
- **Facilities:** Mini-bar, direct-dial phone, alarm clock, satellite TV, Canal+, air-conditioning.
- **Activities on the property:** Swimming pool, 2 tennis courts, sauna, massage on request.
- **Activities in the vicinity:** Golf courses with 9 holes (15 minutes' drive) and 18 holes (25 minutes' drive), horseriding in St Remy or in the Camargue (45 minutes)
- **Sightseeing:** The Lubéron, with exquisite Provençal villages at 30 minutes' drive, Fontaine de Vaucluse, Les Baux, Fontvieille, Eygalières and Arles at 30 minutes, Avignon 20 minutes, Nimes 40 minutes, the Camargue 45 minutes.
- **Credit cards:** Amex, CB, Diners, JCB (Japanese).

Route Départementale 31   p. 10
F. 13210 St Remy-de-Provence
Tel. (33) (0) 4 90/ 92 03 33
Fax. (33) (0) 4 90/ 92 45 17

- **Restaurant:** Very good cuisine, simple but refined, with local produce. Chef Mathias Bettinger (30). Dinner is served on the terrace in the summer, in the restaurant in the winter. Lunch only at the poolside (15/6 - 15/9).
- **Season:** High season from 1/5 to 30/9. Low season from 15/2 to 30/4 and from 1/10 to 15/11.
- **Affiliation:** Châteaux et Hôtels Indépendants and Hostellerie d'Atmosphère. In the hotel guides: Michelin 3 Maisons Rouges, Rivages: hôtel de charme, Gault et Millau.
- **Location:** 2 kilometres from St Remy-de-Provence, in 4 acre parkland. In St Remy take exit Tarascon, Nimes, Arles. After 200 metres, just before the hospital, take the road left D31, then after 1,5 kilometres the hotel is on the right.

HOSTELLERIE DE CRILLON LE BRAVE

- **Room amenities:** 16 rooms and 8 suites (direct phone line, minibar, some rooms with airconditioning)
- **Facilities:** Roomservice, car park, laundry/ dry cleaning
- **Activities on property:** Swimming pool, biking, pétanque
- **Activities in the vicinity:** Tennis, golf, visits to wine cellars
- **Sightseeing:** Orange, Carpentras, Vaison-la-Romaine, Mont Ventoux, Avignon, Lubéron
- **Credit cards:** All major credit cards accepted (except Diners)

Place de l'Eglise   p. 16
F. 84410 Crillon le Brave
Tel. (33) (0) 4 90/ 65 61 61
Fax. (33) (0) 4 90/ 65 62 86

- **Restaurant:** Classical gastronomical cuisine with a provencal accent
- **Season:** Open from mid-March to January 2
- **Affiliation:** Relais & Châteaux
- **Location:** Avignon/ TGV station (30 min), Marseille airport 40 min; 15 kms north of Carpentras (D974 and D138)

CLOÎTRE ST-LOUIS

- **Room amenities:** 72 rooms and 8 suites.
- **Facilities:** Bar, restaurant, conference rooms, garden, terrace, outdoor swimming pool, private parking facilities.
- **Activities on the property:** Outdoor swimming pool (May - October), solarium.
- **Activities in the vicinity:** Avignon and surroundings, places of historic and cultural interest, the vineyards of Côtes du Rhône (Châteauneuf du Pape and others), geological sites (Fontaines de Vaucluse, Gorges de l'Ardèche and du Verdon), Mont Ventoux, Lubéron.

20, Rue Portail Boquier   p. 22
F. 84000 Avignon
Tel. (33) (0) 4 90/ 27 55 55
Fax. (33) (0) 4 90/ 82 24 01

- **Credit cards:** Visa, Amex, JCB, Diners, Mastercard.
- **Restaurant:** Traditional cuisine (closed on Saturdays and Sundays from 1st November to 31st March and closed for lunch on Saturdays and Sundays from 1st April to 31st October, annual holiday in February).
- **Season:** Open all year.
- **Affiliation:** Choice Hotels International (Quality Hotel)
- **Accolades:** Michelin, Gault et Millau.
- **Location:** In the centre of Avignon, 200 m from the station and 500 m from the Palais des Papes.
Follow the signs 'Centre Ville' and 'Gare SNCF'. Opposite station, enter Avignon via Cours Jean-Jaurès.

HOSTELLERIE LA GRANGETTE

Chemin Cambuisson -
Route de Pernes
F. 84740 Velleron
Tel. (33) (0) 4 90/ 20 00 77
Fax. (33) (0) 4 90/ 20 07 06

p. 28

- **Room amenities:** 16.
- **Activities on the property:** Swimming pool, tennis, walking.
- **Activities in the vicinity:** Golf, canoeing, kayak 5 km, horseriding 2km.
- **Sightseeing:** Senanques, Isle-sur-la-Sorgue, Pernes les Fontaines, Carpentras, Gordes, Lubéron, cycling around Sorgues, trekking.
- **Credit cards:** Visa, Amex.

- **Restaurant:** Gastronomic regional cuisine, traditional and popular.
- **Season:** Closed end November to early December and January.
- **Affiliation:** Gault et Millau, Auberges et Hôtels de Charme.
- **Location:** In the countryside, 2 km outside the village. Exit Avignon Nord-Saint - Saturnin les Avignon - Pernes les Fontaines. Direction Isle-sur-Sorgue. D938 Velleron.

LE MOULIN DE LOURMARIN

F. 84160 Lourmarin
Tel. (33) (0) 4 90/ 68 06 69
Fax. (33) (0) 4 90/ 68 31 76

p. 34

- **Rooms:** 18 rooms and 2 suites (direct phone line, private safe,minibar, satellite TV, airconditioning)
- **Facilities:** Roomservice, elevator, English speaking staff, laundry/ dry cleaning service, car park, car rental
- **Activities on property:** Swimming pool, sauna, nature walks with the chef
- **Activities in the vicinity:** Golf (15 min by car), horseback riding, tennis (in the village), helicopter rides, English speaking staff, laundry/ dry cleaning

- **Sightseeing:** Provence, Aix-en-Provence, Avignon, Orange, Vaison-la-Romaine
- **Credit cards:** All major credit cards accepted
- **Restaurant:** Gastronomical and provencal
- **Season:** Open year round
- **Location:** TGV station: Aix-en-Provence 33 km or Avignon 70 km. Airport Marseille/Marignane 50 km

DOMAINE DE CHÂTEAUNEUF

F. 83860 Nans-les-Pins
Tel. (33) (0) 4 94/ 78 90 06
Fax. (33) (0) 4 94/ 78 63 30

p. 40

- **Rooms:** 24 rooms and appartements
- **Activities on property:** Golf (18 holes), swimming pool, tennis, volleyball, pétanque...
- **Sightseeing:** Provence, Aix-en-Provence, Marseille ...
- **Credit cards:** Visa, Amex, JCB, Eurocard - Mastercard, Diners
- **Restaurant:** Provencal cuisine (in the dining room or the courtyard). Wines of Bandol, reknowned Bourgogne & Bordeaux wines

- **Season:** Closed mid-Januar up to end of Februar
- **Location:** Between Aix and Brignoles. Leaving the A7 at St.Maximin, La Sainte Baume, N560, Nans-les-Pins.

LE MAS DE LA FOUQUE

Route du Petit Rhône
F. 13460 Stes-Maries-de-la-Mer
Tel. (33) (0) 4 90/ 97 81 02
Fax. (33) (0) 4 90/ 97 96 84

p. 46

- **Room amenities:** 12 + 2 suites
- **Facilities:** 38 kilometres from Arles, 45 kilometres from Nimes and Montpellier.
- **Activities on the property:** Swimming pool, tennis court, fishing facilities.
- **Activities in the vicinity:** Golf, horseriding, boating.
- **Sightseeing:** Ornithological park, excursion to the Camargue by four-wheel drive.

- **Credit cards:** Visa, Amex, Diners, Mastercard, JCB.
- **Restaurant:** Seats 45, gastronomic and regional cuisine.
- **Season:** 25th March - 2nd November.
- **Affiliation:** ILA, Hôtels de Charme.
- **Accolades:** 4 stars NN, 3 red towers Michelin.
- **Location:** In the heart of the Camargue, surrounded by lakes. RD38 at 4 km from Saintes-Maries, direction Route du Bac Sauvage.

LA BASTIDE

Chemin de Pestelade   p. 52
F. 13810 Eygalières
Tel. (33) (0) 4 90/ 95 90 06
Fax. (33) (0) 4 90/ 95 99 77

- **Room amenities:** 12 rooms, ± 360 FF low season, ± 460 FF high season, breakfast ± 45 FF.
- **Activities on the premises:** Swimming pool, pétanque.
- **Activities in the vicinity:** Tennis, golf, horseriding, walks.
- **Sightseeing:** Les Baux-de-Provence, Arles, Avignon.
- **Credit cards:** Visa, Eurocard, Mastercard.
- **Restaurant:** No..

- **Season:** High season: May - 15th October.
  Low season: 16th October - 15th April.
- **Location:** In the countryside, at the foot of the Alpilles. Autoroute exit Cavaillon, then direction St Remy-de-Provence.

JULES CÉSAR

9, Bd des Lices   p. 56
F. 31631 Arles
Tel. (33) (0) 4 90/ 93 43 20
Fax. (33) (0) 4 90/ 93 33 47

- **Room amenities:** 49 rooms and 5 apartments.
- **Activities on the property:** Tennis, boating, trekking on horseback.
- **Sightseeing:** Les Baux, Provence, Arles and the Camargue.
- **Credit cards:** Visa, Amex, JCB, Eurocard, Mastercard.
- **Restaurant:** 'Lou Marquès', delicious regional specialities and an extrodinary wine list.

- **Season:** Closed from 2nd November to 23rd December.
- **Affiliation:** Relais & Châteaux.
- **Accolades:** Beautiful old convent with cloister gardens
- **Location:** In the centre of Arles.
  From Nîmes: autoroute A54, exit nr. 5, direction Bd G. Clemenceau, then Bd des Lices. Nîmes Airport 25 km, Marseille 80 km.

LA CABRO D'OR

F. 13520 Les Baux de Provence   p. 62
Tel. (33) (0) 4 90/ 54 33 21
Fax. (33) (0) 4 90/ 54 45 98

- **Room amenities:** 31.
- **Activities on the property:** Tennis, swimming pool, horse-drawn carriage rides.
- **Activities in the vicinity:** Golf, horseriding, mountain bike.
- **Sightseeing:** Zoo, Musée de Cheval, villages where santons are made, Musée des Arômes et du Parfum, Cathédrale d'Images, Musée d'antiquités, Château des Baux, Forêt de bambou.

- **Credit cards:** Amex, Visa, Mastercard.
- **Restaurant:** Menus 195 FF, 280 FF, 440 FF + à la carte.
- **Season:** Closed from 11th November to 20th December.
- **Affiliation:** Relais & Châteaux.
- **Location:** In the countryside.
  From A7 exit Cavaillon, direction St Remy, then direction Baux.

ABBAYE
DE SAINTE CROIX

Val de Cuech-Dig   p. 68
F. 13300 Salon de Provence
Tel. (33) (0) 4 90/ 56 24 55
Fax. (33) (0) 4 90/ 56 31 12

- **Room amenities:** 24 rooms, comfort ****, air-conditioning, fully equipped bathrooms, satellite TV.
- **Facilities:** Gastronomic restaurant, 1 Michelin star, Relais & Châteaux.
- **Activities on the property:** Swimming pool, tennis (private club at 300 m), 20 acre park, table tennis.
- **Activities in the vicinity:** Golf 10 km Pont Royal, horseriding 5 km.
- **Sightseeing:** Aix-en-Provence 30 km, Les Baux and Arles 40 km, Avignon and Marseille 45 km.
- **Credit cards:** Visa, Ax, CB, MC, DC.

- **Restaurant:** Gastronomic, 1 star in the Guide Michelin.
- **Season:** Mid-March to the beginning of November.
- **Affiliation:** Relais & Châteaux.
- **Accolades:** 1 star + 3 red houses Michelin, 16/20 Gault et Millau + 2 chef's hats.
- **Location:** High up in the hills, with a wonderful view over the plains of Salon.
  From Aix, Marseille, Lyon and Avignon: A7.
  From Montpellier, Arles: A54. First exit Salon. Follow the arrows in Salon.

CHÂTEAU DE MONTCAUD

Hameau de Combe   p. 74
Route d'Alès (4km)
F. 30200 Bagnols-sur-Cèze
Tel. (33) (0) 4 66/ 89 60 60
Fax. (33) (0) 4 66/ 89 45 04

- **Room amenities:** 29.
- **Facilities:** Mini-bar, satellite TV, restaurant, bar, private park, private attended parking, sauna, steam room, fitness room, bicycle.
- **Activities in the vicinity:** Horseriding (2 km), golf (20 mins), canoeing (15 mins), walks.
- **Sightseeing:** Gorges de l'Ardèche, Pont du Gard, Uzès, Les Cévennes, Avignon, Nîmes, Châteauneuf-du-Pape, Orange.
- **Credit cards:** Visa, Amex, JCB, Eurocard, Mastercard.

- **Restaurant:** Les Jardins de Montcaud.
- **Season:** End March - early November.
- **Affiliation:** Relais et Châteaux.
- **Accolades:** Michelin, Gault et Millau, Bottin Gourmand.
- **Location:** 28 km north-west of Avignon, south of Pont-St-Esprit.
  From the north: A7 exit Bollène, direction Pont-St-Esprit. From the south; A7 exit Avignon-Sud, direction Bagnols-sur-Cèze or A9 exit Remoulins - Bagnols-sur-Cèze.

LE MAS D'ENTREMONT

Route Nationale 7   p. 80
F. 13090 Aix en Provence
Tel. (33) (0) 4 42/ 17 42 42
Fax. (33) (0) 4 42/ 21 15 83

- **Rooms:** 17 rooms and suites (direct phone line, minibar, satellite TV, private safe, airconditioning)
- **Facilities:** Elevator, roomservice, car park, car rent, English speaking staff, laundry/ dry cleaning service
- **Activities on property:** Swimming pool, tennis
- **Activities in the vicinity:** Golf (10 km), horseback rinding (10 km)

- **Sightseeing:** Aix-en-Provence, Provence, Lubéron
- **Credit cards:** All major credit cards accepted
- **Restaurant:** Authentic, aromatic regional cuisine
- **Season:** Closed from 01/11 to 15/03
- **Location:** 30 km from Marseille airport, railway station Aix 4 km

LE MAS DE PEINT

Le Sambuc   p. 86
F. 13200 Arles
Tel. (33) (0) 4 90/ 97 20 62
Fax (33) (0) 4 90/ 97 22 20

- **Rooms:** 8 spacious rooms and 2 suites, all airconditioning (direct phone line, minibar, satellite TV, private safe)
- **Facilities:** Roomservice, car park, car rent Arles, laundry/ dry cleaning service, English speaking staff
- **Activities on property:** 4x4 drive, horseback riding, swimming pool, moutainbike, tours of the property in horse drawn carriage
- **Activities in th vicinity:** Golf (35 km), tennis (25 km)

- **Sightseeing:** Camargue, Arles, Aix-en-Provence, Languedoc
- **Credit cards:** All major credit cards accepted
- **Restaurant:** With home-cooked delicacies featuring own poultry and garden vegetables: light meals by the pool, lunch and dinner served at the kitchen of the mas
- **Season:** Open year round
- **Location:** Arles 25 km, beaches 12 km, airport Nîmes 55 km

HOSTELLERIE LE CASTELLAS

Grand Rue   p. 92
F. 30210 Collias
Tel. (33) (0) 4 66/ 22 88 88
Fax. (33) (0) 4 66/ 22 84 28

- **Room amenities:** 15 rooms, telephone, mini-bar, air-conditioning, 2 suites, TV.
- **Facilities:** Private parking, dry cleaning service.
- **Activities on the premises:** Swimming pool, tennis in the village.
- **Activities in the vicinity:** Horseriding, canoeing, kayak, walks, hikes, swimming, tennis.
- **Sightseeing:** Pont du Gard, Uzès, first duchy of France, Avignon and Nîmes 25 km; Arles, Camargue.

- **Credit cards:** Visa, Diners, JCB, Amex.
- **Restaurant:** Gastronomic cuisine, regional and seasonal.
- **Season:** March to early January.
- **Affiliation:** Châteaux et Hôtels Indépendants.
- **Accolades:** Gault et Millau, Michelin, Champédard, Bottin Gourmand.
- **Location:** In the centre of Collias, 7 km from Pont du Gard et Uzès, 25 km from Avignon and Nîmes. Nîmes Garons Airport 25 km.

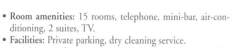

HOSTELLERIE DU VALLON DE VALRUGUES

Chemin Canto Cigalo   p. 98
F. 13210 St Remy-de-Provence
Tel. (33) (0) 4 90/ 92 04 40
Fax. (33) (0) 4 90/ 92 44 01

- **Room amenities:** 53.
- **Facilities:** TV, telephone, safe, mini-bar, air-conditioning, swimming pool.
- **Activities on the premises:** Bar, snooker room, music room, fitness room, sauna, garden, swimming pool, tennis, golf.
- **Activities in the vicinity:** Discovering the Camargue, Arles, Les Baux, the Lubéron, les Alpilles.
- **Sightseeing:** Outings can be organised on request.
- **Credit cards:** CB, AE, DC, JCB, EC.

- **Restaurant:** Gastronomic.
- **Season:** Closed in February.
- **Affiliation:** Small Luxury Hotels.
- **Accolades:** Guide Michelin.
- **Location:** Provençal village near Les Baux-de-Provence (5 mins).
  15 mins from Arles or Avignon Airport.
  35 mins from Marseille Airport.

CHÂTEAU UNANG

Route de Methamis   p. 104
F. 84570 Malemort-du-Comtat
Tel. (33) (0) 4 90/ 69 71 06
Fax. (33) (0) 4 90/ 69 92 85

- **Room amenities:** 4.
- **Facilities:** Large 80 acre estate, rooms with private bathrooms.
- **Activities on the property:** Swimming pool, hiking.
- **Activities in the vicinity:** Golf, tennis, horseriding.
- **Sightseeing:** Avignon, the villages of the Lubéron, Isle-sur-Sorgues, Mont Ventoux, Vaison la Romaine, Châteauneuf-du-Pape...
- * **Credit cards:** Visa, Mastercard.
- * **Restaurant:** Evening meals (reservations only).
- * **Season:** From 1st April to 30th October.

- * **Affiliation:** Châteaux et Hôtels Indépendants, Guide des Chambres d'Hôtes de Charme, Guide des Chambres d'Hôtes de Prestige, Guide des Weekends Amoureux en Provence.
- **Location:** Between Avignon, Vaison and Gordes, in the countryside.
  Exit A7 Avignon-Nord, drive on to Carpentras and then direction Apt (6 km) to roundabout, direction Malemort, then Methamis. Château Unang can be found between two villages on the right.

OUSTAU DE BAUMANIÈRE

F. 13520 Les Baux-de-Provence   p. 110
Tel. (33) (0) 4 90/ 54 33 07
Fax. (33) (0) 4 90/ 54 40 46

- **Room amenities:** 22.
- **Activities on the property:** Tennis, swimming pool, horseriding.
- **Activities in the vicinity:** Day trips, vineyards and wine, olive groves.
- **Sightseeing:** Camargue, Gordes, Bonnieux, Les Baux-de-Provence, oil mills, wine cellars.

- **Credit cards:** American Express, Diners, CB, JCB, Eurocard.
- **Restaurant:** Oustau de Baumanière
- **Season:** Closed from 5th January to 5th March.
- **Affiliation:** Relais & Châteaux, Relais Gourmand.
- **Location:** In the countryside.
  From A7 exit Cavaillon, direction St Remy-de-Provence.

GRAND HÔTEL NORD-PINUS

Place Forum   p. 118
F. 13200 Arles
Tel. (33) (0) 4 90/ 93 44 44
Fax. (33) (0) 4 90/ 93 34 00

- **Rooms:** 22 rooms (direct phone line, satellite TV, private safe, minibar, airconditioning)
- **Facilities:** Roomservice, elevator, car park (garage), car rent, English speaking staff
- **Activities in the vicinity:** Tennis, boat excursions, horseback riding

- **Sightseeing:** Arles, Provence and Camargue, Les Baux
- **Credit cards:** All major credit cards accepted
- **Restaurant:** Provencal cuisine
- **Season:** Open year round
- **Location:** Airport Marseille/ Marignane 50 min, airport Nîmes 25 min, station Arles 5 min

AUBERGE DE CASSAGNE

- **Room amenities:** 25 rooms and 5 suites.
- **Facilities:** Mini-bar, safe, satellite TV, terrace, air-conditioning, bathroom with hairdryer, room service.
- **Activities on the property:** Swimming pool, tennis, jacuzzi, table tennis, pétanque.
- **Activities in the vicinity:** Horseriding, golf, bowling, karting, walks, mountain biking.
- **Sightseeing:** Avignon, St Remy-de-Provence, Les Baux, Mont Ventoux, Isle-sur-la-Sorgue, Gordes, Roussillon, Arles.

450 Allée de Cassagne   p. 122
F. 84130 Le Pontet-Avignon
Tel. (33) (0) 4 90/ 31 04 18
Fax. (33) (0) 4 90/ 32 25 09

- **Credit cards:** Visa, Amex, JCB, Eurocard, Diners, Mastercard.
- **Restaurant:** Gastronomic restaurant with Michelin star.
- **Season:** Open all year.
- **Affiliation:** Romantik Hotel, Relais du Silence, Châteaux et Hôtels Indépendants.
- **Location:** 10 mins from the centre of Avignon, 10 mins péage Avignon-Nord, 10 mins Avignon Airport.
  A7: exit Avignon-Nord.
  A9: direction Carpentras, Le Pontet, then road to Vedène.

MARIE D'AGOULT - CHÂTEAU D'ARPAILLARGUES

- **Room amenities:** 27 rooms and 2 apartments.
- **Facilities:** Park and garden. 6 ground floor rooms
- **Activities on the property:** Swimming pool, tennis.
- **Activities in the vicinity:** Golf, kayak, balloon flights, horseriding.
- **Sightseeing:** Pont du Gard, Uzès, Nîmes, Avignon, Arles, the Camargue.
- **Credit cards:** Visa, Amex, Mastercard.
- **Restaurant:** Refined local cuisine.

F. 30700 Uzès   p. 128
Tel. (33) (0) 4 66/ 22 14 48
Fax. (33) (0) 4 66/ 22 56 10

- **Season:** End of March to the end of October.
- **Affiliation:** Relais du Silence, Châteaux et Hôtels Indépendants, Hôtels Particuliers.
- **Accolades:** 3 stars NN, Michelin.
- **Location:** 4 km from Uzès (road to Anduze) just outside the village.
  From Lyon: Remoulins - Uzès - Arpaillargues.
  From Marseille: Arles - Nîmes Ouest - Alès - Uzès.
  From Montpellier: Nîmes Ouest - Alès - Uzès.

HÔTEL DU GÉNÉRAL D'ENTRAIGUES

- **Room amenities:** 19.
- **Facilities:** Lift, outdoor swimming pool, terraces with greenery, lounge, bar.
- **Activities on the property:** Swimming pool.
- **Activities in the vicinity:** Golf, kayak, mountain biking, horseriding.
- **Sightseeing:** Pont du Gard, le Duché, Uzès, Nîmes, Arles, the Cévennes.
- **Credit cards:** Visa, Amex, Mastercard, Diners.

Place de l'Evèche   p. 128
F. 30700 Uzès
Tel. (33) (0) 4 66/ 22 32 68
Fax. (33) (0) 4 66/ 22 57 01

- **Restaurant:** Traditional gastronomic cuisine.
- **Season:** Open all year.
- **Affiliation:** Les Hôtels Particuliers.
- **Accolades:** 3 stars NN.
- **Location:** Uzès, Place de l'Evéché (in the centre of town).
  From Avignon: Remoulins - Uzès.
  From Montpellier: Nîmes Ouest - Alès - Uzès.

HOSTELLERIE LES FRÊNES

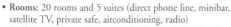

- **Rooms:** 20 rooms and 5 suites (direct phone line, minibar, satellite TV, private safe, airconditioning, radio)
- **Facilities:** Roomservice, car park, laundry/ dry cleaning, elevator, car rent, English speaking staff
- **Activities on property:** Swimming pool, jacuzzi, sauna
- **Activities in the vicinity:** Horseback riding ,tennis, golf, biking
- **Sightseeing:** Avignon, Provence, Camargue

645, Avenue des Vertes-Rives   p. 134
F. 84140 Montfavet/ Avignon
Tel. (33) (0) 4 90/ 31 17 93
Fax. (33) (0) 4 90/ 23 95 03

- **Credit cards:** All major credit cards accepted
- **Restaurant:** Classical gastronomical cuisine with a provencal accent
- **Season:** Open from the beginning of april to the end of october
- **Affiliation:** Relais & Châteaux
- **Location:** Avignon TGV station 10 min, Marseille airport 1 h

HOSTELLERIE
CHÂTEAU DE LA PIOLINE

- **Room amenities:** 18 rooms and 3 suites (direct phone line, satellite TV, airconditioning)
- **Facilities:** Room service, English speaking staff, car park, car rent, laundry/ dry cleaning, theatre reservations
- **Activities:** Swimming pool
- **Activities in the vicinity:** Tennis, golf (3 kms), horseback riding
- **Sightseeing:** Aix-en-Provence, and excursions in the Provence

F. 13290 Aix-en-Provence   p. 140
Tel. (33) (0) 4 42/ 20 07 81
Fax. (33) (0) 4 42/ 59 96 12

- **Credit cards:** All major credit cards accepted
- **Restaurant:** Reknowned, authentic regional cuisine
- **Season:** Open year round
- **Affiliation:** Châteaux & Hôtels Indépendants
- **Location:** 3 kms from Aix downtown, 30 min by car from Marseille/ Marignane airport, Aix railway station 3 kms

LES ROCHES

- **Room amenities:** 35 rooms and 5 apartments with sea view, direct-dial phone, mini-bar, air-conditioning, hairdryer.
- **Facilities:** Parking facilities, car rental, dry cleaning service.
- **Activities on the property:** Swimming pool, kayaks, diving lessons, boat hire.
- **Activities in the vicinity:** Golf (10 km), tennis (3 km), horseriding (10 km), all watersports (3 km).
- **Sightseeing:** Iles d'Or (Porquerolles, Port Cros), Hyères, Bormes-les-Mimosas, Saint-Tropez.

1, Avenue de Trois Dauphins,   p. 146
Aiguebelle
F. 83380 Le Lavandou
Tel. (33) (0) 4 94/ 71 05 07
Fax. (33) (0) 4 94/ 71 08 40

- **Credit cards:** All major credit cards.
- **Restaurant:** Gastronomic: refined regional cuisine.
- **Season:** End March to mid-October.
- **Affiliation:** Relais & Châteaux.
- **Location:** In a calanque by the sea, fully equipped private beach.
  Toulon Airport, Hyères 30 mins. Marseille/Marignane Airport 1.30 hrs. Nice Airport 2 hrs.

AUBERGE DE NOVES

- **Room amenities:** 19 rooms and 4 apartments junior suites.
- **Facilities:** Special facilities for handicapped people. Lift. Free private parking facilities. Laundry and dry cleaning service.
- **Activities on the property:** Tennis, table tennis, swimming pool, mountain biking, walks on the 15 acre estate, straight from the hotel.
- **Activities in the vicinity:** Horseriding (5 km), golf (3 courses in an area of 30 km), hunting, fishing.
- **Sightseeing:** Avignon, Orange, Châteauneuf-du-Pape, les Alpilles, the Lubéron, Isle-sur-la-Sorgue, the Camargue.
- **Credit cards:** American Express, Diners, Visa, Mastercard, JCB, Eurocard.

Domaine de Deves   p. 152
Route de Châteaurenard
F. 13550 Noves
Tel. (33) (0) 4 90/ 24 28 28
Fax. (33) (0) 4 90/ 24 28 00

- **Restaurant:** Dining room, winter lounge and covered terrace in the summer.
- **Season:** Open all year.
- **Affiliation:** Relais & Châteaux.
- **Accolades:** 1 star Michelin, 2 towers, Gault et Millau, 2 stars Bottin Gourmand - red towers Michelin.
- **Location:** Avignon Airport 7 km, TGV station Avignon 15 km, Marseille Airport 65 km.
  From A7 exit Avignon-Sud in the direction of Aix-Marseille then towards Châteaurenard.

LA BASTIDE
DE CAPELONGUE

- **Rooms:** 17
- **Facilities:** 1 room equipped for persons with a handicap
- **Activities on property:** Swimming pool
- **Activities in the vicinity:** Tennis, golf, mountainbike
- **Sightseeing:** Villages in the Lubéron, museums
- **Credit cards:** CB,EC,Visa, AE, DC
- **Restaurant:** Yes

F. 84480 Bonnieux   p. 158
Tel. (33) (0) 4 90/ 75 89 78
Fax. (33) (0) 4 90/ 75 93 03

- **Season:** Open mid-March - mid-November
- **Affiliation:** Relais & Châteaux
- **References:** Gault et Millau, Michelin
- **Location:** Panoramic view on Bonnieux, in the heart of the Lubéron. Leaving the A7 in Avignon-sud, then N100.

VILLA GALLICI

- **Rooms:** 22 rooms and appartments, all with aircon-ditioning (satellite TV, minibar, direct phone line, safe, radio)
- **Facilities:** Roomservice, English speaking staff, laundry/dry cleaning, car park, car rent
- **Activities on property:** Swimming pool
- **Activities in the vicinity:** Sauna, health club, tennis, golf, horseback riding, biking, organized walks
- **Sightseeing:** Aix-en-Provence, the Provence, the Lubéron, the Calanques

- **Credit cards:** All major credit cards accepted
- **Restaurant:** Provencal cuisine (only for residents)
- **Season:** Open all year round
- **Affiliation:** Relais & Châteaux
- **Location:** 5min walk from center of Aix, 30min by car from Marseille airport, 10min by car from the railway station. In the center of Aix, just follow signs "Villa Gallici"

RELAIS DE LA MAGDELEINE

- **Room amenities:** 24.
- **Facilities:** Room service, private parking, car rental, dry cleaning, lift.
- **Activities on the premises:** Swimming pool, walks.
- **Activities in the vicinity:** Horseriding (1 km), golf (10 km), tennis (1 km).
- **Sightseeing:** The calanques of Cassis, Aix-en-Provence, Victoire Ste Baume.

- **Credit cards:** Visa, Mastercard.
- **Restaurant:** Yes.
- **Season:** 15th March - 1st December.
- **Affiliation:** Châteaux et Hôtels Indépendants.
- **Accolades:** Michelin, Gault et Millau, Bottin Gourmand.
- **Location:** Marseille Marignane Airport 35 mins.

LA MIRANDE

- **Rooms:** 19 rooms and 1 suite (direct phone line, minibar, satellite TV, private safe, airconditioning)
- **Facilities:** Elevator, roomservice, car park, laundry/ dry cleaning, English speaking staff
- **Activities on property:** Courses in gastronomy, jazz club, concerts classical music
- **Sightseeing:** Avignon, Provence, Camargue

- **Credit cards:** All major credit cards accepted
- **Restaurant:** French gastronomical cuisine with a provencal accent
- **Season:** Open all year round
- **Affiliation:** Small Luxury hotels
- **Location:** Downtown Avignon. TGV station 5 min, airport Marseille 1h

LE MAS DE L'OULIVIÉ

- **Room amenities:** 22 rooms and 1 suite, all with air-conditioning, telephone, mini-bar, safe, TV.
- **Facilities:** Private parking space, car rental, dry cleaning, money change.
- **Activities on the property:** Tennis, swimming pool, walks in the Alpilles.
- **Activities in the vicinity:** Golf (2 km), horseriding (1 km), mountain bikes, four-wheel drive excursions in the Camargue.
- **Sightseeing:** Baux-de-Provence, St Remy-de-Provence, Avignon, Arles and the Camargue.

- **Credit cards:** All major credit cards.
- **Restaurant:** Provençal specialities, served by the pool at lunchtime.
- **Season:** Closed from mid-November to mid-March.
- **Affiliation:** Châteaux et Hôtels Indépendants.
- **Location:** Avignon Airport 35 km, Nîmes 45 km, Marseille 60 km. TGV station/Arles 15 km.
  A7 exit Avignon-Sud, exit A54 St Martin-de-Crau, D78 direction Fontvielle.

LE MAS DE LA BRUNE

F. 13810 Eygalières   p. 190
Tel. (33) (0) 4 90/ 95 90 77
Fax. (33) (0) 4 90/ 95 99 21

- **Room amenities:** 9 rooms, 1 apartment.
- **Facilities:** Private parking, dry cleaning.
- **Activities on the premises:** Outdoor swimming pool, quiet park and garden open to visitors.
- **Activities in the vicinity:** Golf 20 km.
- **Sightseeing:** St Remy-de-Provence, Arles, Avignon, Les Baux.
- **Credit cards:** Visa, Eurocard, Mastercard.

- **Restaurant:** No..
- **Season:** Closed 15th December - 15th January.
- **Affiliation:** Châteaux et Hôtels Indépendants.
- **Accolades:** Gault et Millau, Michelin.
- **Location:** In the middle of the Alpilles, 25 kms from Avignon, Marseille Airport 45 km, Nîmes and Arles 50 km. A7 exit Cavaillon, then D99 direction St Remy-de-Provence.

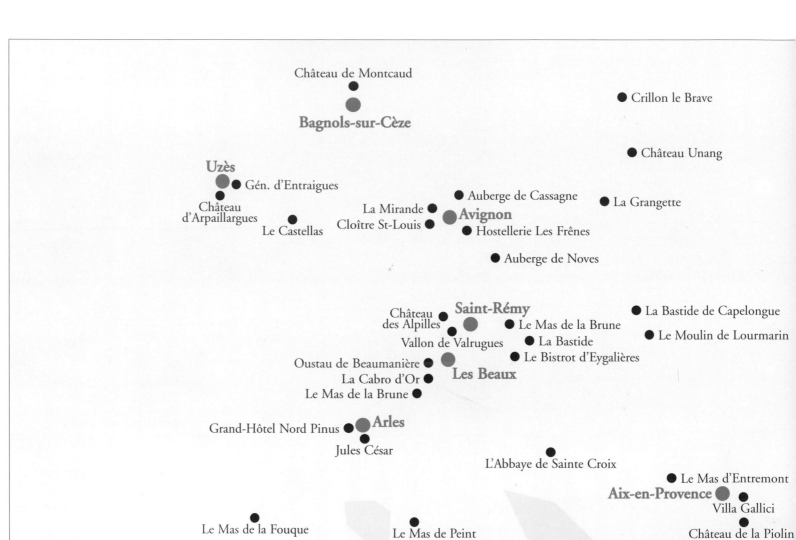

LE BISTROT D'EYGALIÈRES

Rue de la République   p. 196
F. 13810 Eygalières
Tel. (33) (0) 4 90/ 90 60 34
Fax (33) (0) 4 90/ 90 60 37

- **Credit cards:** Visa, Eurocard, Mastercard, CB.
- **Restaurant:** 1 Michelin star. Specialities: noix coquilles St-Jacques crues marinées, crème de tourteaux, pommes poêlées aux truffes, foie de canard poêlé au vinaigre balsamique, rouleau de pigeon aux échalotes confites, mille-feuilles aux chocolats, mousse d'orange, fraises des bois.
- **Season:** easter to mid-October.

- **Affiliation:** Gault et Millau, Michelin, Bottin Gourmand, Guide Hubert.
- **Accolades:** 1 star Michelin.
- **Location:** In the centre of the village.
  A7 Lyon- Avignon - exit Cavaillon, then RN99 direction St Remy-de-Provence, 10 km to Eygalières, centre of the village.

Les Roches
●

LIST OF PHOTOGRAPHERS

Ditmar Bollaert: Le Moulin de Lourmarin, Le Mas d'Entremont, Hostellerie Les Frênes, Château de la Pioline, Les Roches, La Bastide de Capelongue, Le Relais de la Magdeleine.

Vincent Gyselinck: Hostelerie La Grangette, Domaine de Châteauneuf, La Bastide, Château Unang, Auberge de Noves, La Mirande, Le Mas de la Brune.

Patrick Verbeeck: Château des Alpilles, Hostellerie de Crillon le Brave, Cloître St-Louis, Le Mas de la Fouque, Jules César, La Cabro d'Or, L'Abbaye de Ste Croix, Château de Montcaud, Le Mas de Peint, Hostellerie de Vallon de Valrugues, Oustau de Beaumanière, Grand-Hôtel Nord Pinus, Auberge de Cassagne, Château d'Arpaillargues & Gén. d'Entraigues, Le Mas de l'Oulivié, Le Bistrot d'Eygalières.

Eric Morin: Villa Gallici.

Francis Vuillemin: Hostellerie Le Castellas.